MEMORIAL DAY

by Robin Nelson

first step nonfiction

Lerner Publications Company · Minneapolis

We **celebrate** Memorial Day every year.

May

Sunday	Monday	Tuesday	Wednesday	Thursday	Friday	Saturday
			1	2	3	4
5	6	7	8	9	10	11
12	13	14	15	16	17	18
19	20	21	22	23	24	25
26	27	28	29	30	31	

This holiday is in May.

3

Memorial Day began
many years ago.

People wanted to **honor soldiers** who had died.

People **decorated graves.**

They had parades.

Today we remember all
people who have died.

We celebrate Memorial Day in many ways.

Many towns still have
parades.

We still remember people
who have died in wars.

People decorate graves
with flowers and flags.

People go to a place of worship.

We celebrate the
beginning of summer.

Families have picnics.

On Memorial Day, we honor
those who have died.

We celebrate and
remember.

Memorial Day Timeline

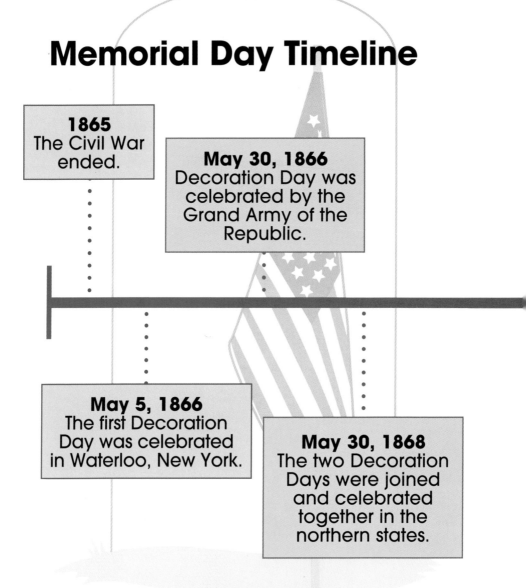

1865
The Civil War ended.

May 30, 1866
Decoration Day was celebrated by the Grand Army of the Republic.

May 5, 1866
The first Decoration Day was celebrated in Waterloo, New York.

May 30, 1868
The two Decoration Days were joined and celebrated together in the northern states.

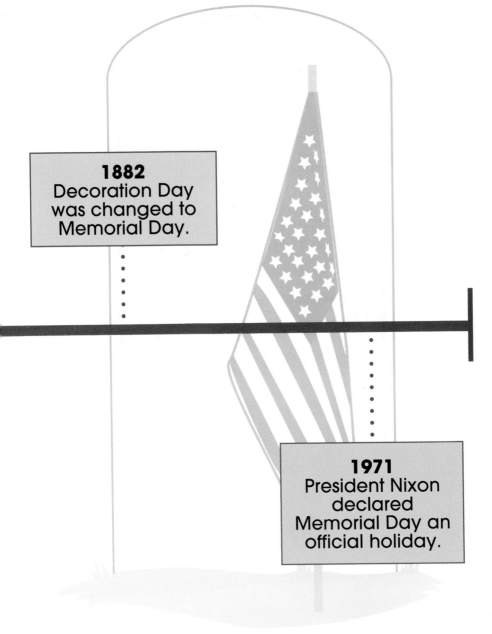

1882
Decoration Day was changed to Memorial Day.

1971
President Nixon declared Memorial Day an official holiday.

Memorial Day Facts

 Memorial Day began during the Civil War. During this war, Americans from the Southern states fought Americans from the Northern states. They were fighting over whether the United States should stay one country.

 The first Memorial Day was actually called Decoration Day. It was celebrated on May 5, 1866 in Waterloo, New York.

We raise American flags only halfway up the flagpole as a way to honor those who have died.

 Navy sailors throw flowers into the ocean to remember the dead.

 Soldiers at army bases fire their rifles into the air to honor those who have died.

Glossary

 celebrate – to have a party or special activity to honor a special occasion

 decorated – placed something beautiful on

 graves – places where people are buried after they die

 honor – to show special respect for

 soldiers – members of an army

Index

The photographs in this book are reproduced through the courtesy of: © Diane Meyer, front cover, pp. 2, 8, 9, 16, 17, 22 (top, middle, and bottom); © Todd Strand/ Independent Picture Service, p. 3; © Northwind Picture Archives, pp. 4, 5, 6, 7, 22 (second from top and second from bottom); © Betty Crowell, pp. 10, 11, 12, 14, 15; © Robert Fried, p. 13.

This book is available in two editions:
Library binding by Lerner Publications Company, a division of Lerner Publishing Group, Inc.
Soft cover by First Avenue Editions, an imprint of Lerner Publishing Group, Inc.
241 First Avenue North
Minneapolis, MN 55401 USA

For reading levels and more information, look up this title at www.lernerbooks.com.

Library of Congress Cataloging-in-Publication Data

Nelson, Robin, 1971–
    Memorial Day / by Robin Nelson.
        p.   cm. — (First step nonfiction)
    Includes index.
    Summary: A simple introduction to why and how we celebrate Memorial Day.
    ISBN 978–0–8225–1273–8 (lib. bdg. : alk. paper)
    ISBN 978–0–8225–1317–9 (pbk. : alk. paper)
    ISBN 978–0–8225–8006–5 (eBook)
    1. Memorial Day—Juvenile literature. [1. Memorial Day. 2. Holidays.]
    I. Title. II. Series.
    E642.N45 2003
    394.262—dc21   2001007835

Manufactured in China
7 – SS – 1/1/14